Fighting Words

Prayers Against
Mental Illness & Diseases

Fighting Words

Prayers Against
Mental Illness & Diseases

Okisha L. Jackson

asf.bookseries@aol.com
www.twitter.com/SheNevaStuck

All Scripture quotations are from the Message Bible, NLT, and the King James Version of the Bible. All references are cited for each disorder & disease from the Internet.

Print version format by Okisha Jackson
Editing by Okisha Jackson
Printing by CreateSpace, An Amazon Company
Book Cover Design (2017) by Ebook Launch
Fighting Words/ Okisha Jackson. -- 1st Ed.
ISBN 13: 978-0-692-90103-8

Dedications

I dedicate this book to *God my Heavenly Father, Jesus my Savior, and my helper the Holy Spirit.* Lord, thank you for trusting me to do this and giving me this idea to put out to people. I hope it accomplishes more than can I could hope for and heal the people that get and pray this book. I give you all the glory, honor, and praise.

-*Momma*, you retired as a Master Sergeant from the United States Army. You were and still is a champion and a hero to everyone who has come into contact with you- who didn't get on your bad side. There's not enough words or actions to show you that I appreciate and love you very much.

-*Raphael*, you've come along way son. We may have had a rough start, but I'm believing God for you to have a great finish. You can achieve anything you want to if you go after it with all your mind and strength.

-*Peter*, you are a walking miracle son. Always remember it was God that has brought you through and is the one blessing you. Give him the praise and thank him every day.

-*Elijah*, you have a big little heart son. Thank you for your consideration, laughter, and fun. You are also smart. Don't forget you are called to preach the gospel.

Greetings,

In the precious name of the Lord Jesus.

This book is written for Christians, prayer warriors, and believers who understand the warfare in the spiritual realm that has manifested in this dimension.

We know illnesses and diseases just doesn't pop out of the nowhere and that Satan, our adversary, is a legalist. Where there is sin, un-forgiveness, & no repentance there's a multitude of open doors of attack that his demons unleash on humans from generation to generations and they have.

Some of you may want to know why all the prayers start off the same way. The reason why every prayer starts off with repentance and re-dedication is because Satan is a legalist, as I've mentioned before. You can't go to gun fight with a sword. You got to be clean and geared for the fight because if any enemy sees that you're not in the right position they will come after you and take you down for even trying.

This book was written by the inspiration of the Holy Spirit to bring the practical knowledge of medicine and prayer to our creator together.

Doctors can only go so far, but God created us so, He's the only one that can fix us.

There are only a few mental illnesses & diseases the Lord had me put in here because this is my lane. I've got to stay in the lane the Lord has anointed me to be in.

I hope you are fasted and prayed up before you read these prayers for others and be led by the Holy Spirit so, you can be in your lane and operate according to the anointing He has ordained you with.

You ready?

Get set ....fight!!!

Contents

Depression

http://www.healthline.com/health/depression/effects-brain#2

According to Erica Cirino, depression is a mood disorder that effects the way you think, feel, and behave (2016).

Long term depression is known as clinical depression or major depressive disorder (MDD). While others may suffer from it a few times in their life (Cirino, 2016).

The symptoms of MDD significantly interfere with daily activities, such as: school, work, and social events. They also impact mood and behavior as well as various physical functions, such as sleep and appetite. To be diagnosed with MDD, you must display five or more of the following symptoms at least once a day over the course of two weeks:

- persistent feelings of sadness and hopelessness
- lack of interest in doing most activities, including those you once enjoyed
- decrease or increase in appetite accompanied by extreme weight loss or weight gain
- sleeping too much or too little
- restlessness
- fatigue
- excessive or inappropriate feelings of guilt or worthlessness
- difficulty making decisions, thinking, and concentrating
- multiple thoughts of death or suicide

- A suicide attempt (Cirino, 2016).

  Researchers believe depression is generational. That people with a family history of MDD are more likely to develop the disorder than others.

- **Stress**: A stressful life event, such a divorce or death of a loved one, can trigger an episode of MDD.
- **Biochemical reactions**: Chemicals in the brains of people with MDD seem to function differently than those in the brains of those without the disorder.
- **Hormone imbalances**: Changes in the balance of hormones may trigger MDD in certain people, especially during menopause or during and after pregnancy.

There are three parts of the brain that appear to play a major role in MDD: the hippocampus, amygdala, and prefrontal cortex (Cirino, 2016).

Fight

Heavenly Father we come to you in the name of Jesus your son. I ask you to please forgive and cleanse me from all my sins. Jesus I re-dedicate my life to you and ask you to be my Savior in every area of life right now and I know, confess, and believe with all my heart that you're the Son of God and died for the sins of the world.

Jesus, son of the most-high God, please equip me with the armor you know I will need to fight against the spirit of depression. Please enable us to operate according to the rank in your army Jesus you have called us to and grant us divine, supernatural protection for me, every one assigned, and related to me from all demonic counter-attacks.

Lord God of Heaven, we ask you for forgiveness for the people who opened the door to the sins that caused this brain disorder/disease of depression, to be passed down from generation to generation. Lord, this person was born into this curse, _____ is innocent. We ask you for a full pardon from this curse that was imputed into him/her from the time of conception and ask for total healing & deliverance please in the name of your Holy Son Jesus according to John 16:23.

Father God in Heaven & Jesus, we lift up _____ right now to you. We ask you Jesus to be our sword of the spirit. To supply your anointing & power and blood to destroy everything that falls under the host & gods of depression, suicide, heaviness, un-forgiveness & murder. Also to uproot the chains of the situation that caused it to develop in the first place. To remove every trigger that causes all the symptoms of all types of depression to activate. To rectify, heal, and regulate the hippocampus, amygdala, hormone & ph balances within the body, biochemical reactions, and prefrontal cortex according to your optimum divine design.

We bind & loose all of these things from _____ central nervous system and all their functions in the name of Jesus according to Matthew 16:19 and send every trace of their existence straightway to the pit of hell with no replacements.

Jesus please loose into _____ regulated levels of cortisol in the frontal lobe part of the brain, proper levels and flow of serotonin, norepinephrine, dopamine, and healthy brain cell communication. Lord Jesus please seal all ___ deliverances and this entire prayer in your blood.

Heavenly Father, we ask you for total restoration of every blessing that the devil stole from _____ that he/she doesn't even know about. That this person now lives the abundant life your son Jesus Christ suffered and died for _____ to have immediately please in the name of Jesus Christ of Nazareth we pray and ask for all of these things to be done according to John 16:23 amen.

Pornography

Facts I believe are true. You can read them from this website. Download the pdf and read page 432.

http://www.genemoody.com/uploads/9/3/7/9/93799862/the_complete_deliverance_manual_by_gene_moody.pdf

People who watch and read pornographic material grow up to be men & women who most likely ...

- Will not see the need to provide financially or spiritually for their spouse and children.

- Often hates the spouse and children, and feels they hamper him/her.

- Does not understand responsibilities for the family, neither cares.

- Usually will not hold a steady job.

- Burdened by tormenting fear.

Fight

Heavenly Father we come to you in the name of Jesus your son. I ask you to please forgive and cleanse me from all my sins. Jesus I re-dedicate my life to you and ask you to be my Savior in every area of life right now and I know, confess, and believe with all my heart that you're the Son of God.

Please equip me with the armor you know I will need to fight against the hosts of pornography. Please enable us to operate according to the rank in your army Jesus you have called us to and grant us divine, supernatural protection for me, every one assigned, and related to me from all demonic counter-attacks.

We lift up _____ to you Heavenly Father and lock his/her flesh down that there's no access to the kingdom of darkness. We put every area of carnality, the three gates and nineteen doors of ____ soul under submission to the blood of Jesus Christ of Nazareth right now in the name of Jesus.

We ask you Jesus to supply your anointing, glory, and power to put all the functions of the conscious, pituitary gland, temporal lobe, occipital lobe, all sensory glands, all reproductive organs, and subconscious parts of ____ brain and body parts under the authority and blood of Jesus Christ of Nazareth right now and submerge____ spirit in the fire of the Holy Ghost according to Luke 3:22.

We place the blood of Jesus between the enemies that's fighting against _____ in the name of Jesus Christ we pray according to John 14:13-14.

Jesus, son of the most high God, we ask you to bind & loose (Matthew 16:19) and supply your anointing power, & glory to destroy everything that falls under the host and gods of perversion, incubus & succubus, and everything that's been loosed & poured out over the entire nation of America from the year 2015 and all its seeds planted from demonic dreams, visions, imaginations, engagements and demonic sexual encounters in the spiritual realm, and we ask you Jesus, our commander-in-chief, to destroy all of their signs, symptoms, manifestations, effects, adverse effects, stings, wrong mind sets, emotions, attacks, coming in and against _____ and in the heavenlies completely please.

Lord Jesus please seal ___ deliverances and this entire prayer in your blood.

We ask you Heavenly Father, the righteous judge, the Alpha and Omega, to hover your foot over ___ to fully terminate & remove this assignment from ___ life without the ability to be re-assigned another specialty. That their banned from the planet earth and all humans, sentenced to the pit of hell until their final place in the lake of fire in the name of Jesus Christ of Nazareth.

Heavenly Father, we ask you to restore every blessing the devil stole from ___, heavenly relationships, healthy relationships, favor, fun, joy, peace, laughter, prosperity, good health, right mind, protection, contentment, humility, heart of a servant, gifts, anointing, praise, self- control, worship, every promise written in the Bible, and the abundant life your son Jesus Christ suffered and died for _____ to have right now please in the name of Jesus Christ of Nazareth we pray and ask all for all of these things to be done according to John 16:23 amen.

ADHD/ADD

You can review slide 9, 10, 13, 19, & 20

https://www.slideshare.net/CMoondog/adhd-and-thebrain

Here are a few internal/external issues that goes on with a person with ADHD.

- Lack of regulation of attention, motor activity, and impulsivity.
- Probable area affected by the brain are: frontal lobes/prefrontal cortex, limbic system, basal ganglia.

- Having too much or too little of Dopamine affects how the basal ganglia communicates to the brain.
- People with ADHD have disturbances in the <u>dopamine system</u> innervating the basal ganglia and the frontal lobes. The lack of dopamine makes it difficult for someone with ADHD to pay attention to non-stimulating activities. It's not that people with ADHD are over stimulated rather they are under stimulated (Forssberg et al. (2006) Armstrong (2010).
- <u>Norepinephrine</u> is a neurotransmitter that is responsible for moving nerve impulses between neurons. Acting as a neurotransmitter, norepinephrine's role is for arousal and attentiveness. A lack of norepinephrine causes issue's with attention and emotional responses (Sweeney, 2009).

- <u>Glutamate</u> is also a neurotransmitter and its role is important to learning and memory. Small quantities of glutamate however can have damaging effects by killing neurons (Sweeny, 2009).

Fight

Holy Spirit please pray with me and through me.
Heavenly Father we come to you in the name of
Jesus your son. I ask you to please forgive and
cleanse me from all my sins. Jesus I re-dedicate my
life to you and ask you to be my Savior in every area
of life right now and I know, confess, and believe
with all my heart that you're the Son of God.

Please equip me with the armor you know I will need
to fight against the generational curse of ADHD.
Please enable us to operate according to the rank in
your army Jesus you have called us to and grant us
divine, supernatural protection for me, every one
assigned, and related to me from all demonic
counter-attacks.

**Lord God of Heaven, we ask you for forgiveness
for the people who opened the door to the sins
that caused this brain disorder/disease ADHD, to
be passed down from generation to generation.
Lord, this person was born into this curse, ____ is
innocent. We ask you for a full pardon from this
curse that was imputed into him/her from the
time of conception and ask for total healing &
deliverance please in the name of your Holy Son
Jesus according to John 16:23.**

We lift up _____ to you Heavenly Father and come in
agreement with the anointing, power, glory, wisdom,
judgment, miracles, and testimonies of everything
that you created throughout the universe that gives
you praise and that's written in the Holy Bible.

We come in agreement with every prayer warrior
that's in right standing with you Father God of
Heaven for more power, we come in agreement with

every anointed word that's been preached, and every form of Christian ministry from the beginning of time even until now that are and has been approved, called, chosen, sanctified, and accepted by you Heavenly Father in the name of Jesus. Lord Jesus we come in agreement with your baptism, the test you passed in the wilderness, and your resurrection for more power to get the victory immediately for the person were believing you for according to John 16:23 Father God.

Jesus, thou Son of David, we ask you to supply your anointing, power, and glory to heal, regulate, formulate the chemicals of dopamine, norepinephrine, glutamate, in the frontal lobes/prefrontal cortex, limbic system, and basal ganglia. Proper alignment & brain cell communication between every nerve cell, and full removal of all disturbances within the dopamine system and to fill the triad chemicals of dopamine, norepinephrine, and glutamate to their proper levels to rectify the flow & stimulation necessary to function accordingly to your optimum divine design.

We ask you Heavenly Father, the righteous judge, The Alpha and Omega, to hover your foot over ___ to fully terminate & remove the host of adhd from their assignments on ___ life without the ability to be re-assigned another specialty.

That their banned from the planet earth and all humans, sentenced to the pit of hell until their final place in the lake of fire in the name of Jesus Christ of Nazareth.

Lord Jesus please seal ___ deliverances and this entire prayer in your blood.

Heavenly Father, we ask you to restore every blessing that the devil stole from ____ that they don't even know about, every blessing, heavenly relationship, favor, prosperity, good health, right mind, protection, gifts, anointing, peace, healthy relationships, joy, fun, laughter, humor, praise, contentment, worship, humility, heart of a servant, every promise written in the Bible, and the abundant life your son Jesus Christ suffered and died for ____ to have right now please in the name of Jesus Christ of Nazareth we pray and ask for all of these things to be done according to John 16:23 amen.

Autism

http://www.thebrainperformancecenter.com/conditions-and-symptoms/autism-spectrum/

- *Autism* spectrum disorder (ASD) and **autism** are both general terms for a group of complex disorders of brain development. People with <u>autism</u> often have underdeveloped brain structures, mainly the amygdala and the hippocampus, which is the structure involved in emotion, aggression, sensory input, memory, and learning.

- It is hypothesized that because of the underdeveloped system, many autistic children have problems integrating sensory information, and are over or under stimulated.
- The cause of autism is still not known, but is heavily linked to genetic disruptions during the time of conception.

Fight

Holy Spirit please pray with me and through me. Heavenly Father we come to you in the name of Jesus your son. I ask you to please forgive and cleanse me from all my sins. Jesus I re-dedicate my life to you and ask you to be my Savior in every area of life right now and I know, confess, and believe with all my heart that you're the Son of God.

Please equip me with the armor you know I will need to fight against the generational curse of Autism. Please enable us to operate according to the rank in your army Jesus you have called us to and grant us divine, supernatural protection for me, every one assigned, and related to me from all demonic counter-attacks.

Lord God of Heaven, we ask you for forgiveness for the persons who caused the door to the sins that caused this brain disorder/disease Autism, to be passed down from generation to generation. Lord, this person was born into this curse, ____ is innocent. We ask you for a full pardon from this curse that was imputed into him/her from the time of conception and ask for total healing & deliverance please in the name of your Holy Son Jesus according to John 16:23.

Lord Jesus, son of the most high God, we ask you to bestow your anointing, glory, and power upon ___ to rectify his/her underdeveloped brain structures, mainly the amygdala and the hippocampus, and all the structural functions involved in emotion, aggression, sensory input, memory, and learning neurofeedback. To heal all the problems & disturbances of brain dysregulation. Please enable proper flow of integrating sensory information, and secure the correct levels of chemicals to bring the normal balance of stimulation.

We ask you Heavenly Father, the righteous judge, The Alpha and Omega, to hover your foot over ___ to fully terminate & remove everything that falls under the host of autism & their assignments on ___ life without the ability to be re-assigned another specialty.

That their banned from the planet earth and all humans, sentenced to the pit of hell until their final place in the lake of fire in the name of Jesus Christ of Nazareth.

Lord Jesus please seal ___ deliverances and this entire prayer in your blood.

Heavenly Father, we ask you to restore every blessing that the devil stole from ___ that they don't even know about, every blessing, heavenly relationship, favor, prosperity, clarity and focus in the mind, sharp attention to detail, the spirit of a finisher, the spirit of a winner, the heart of a servant, true humility, integrity, honesty, loyalty only to good things in the mind of ___ , good health, right mind, protection, gifts, anointing, peace, healthy relationships, joy, fun, laughter, humor, praise, contentment, worship, humility, heart of a servant, every promise written in the Bible, and the abundant life your son Jesus Christ suffered and died for ___ to have right now please in the name of Jesus Christ of Nazareth we pray and ask for all of these things to be done according to John 16:23 amen.

Prescription Drug Addiction

http://www.mayoclinic.org/diseasesconditions/prescription-drugabuse/basics/definition/con-20032471

According to the Mayo Clinic, prescription drug abuse is the **use of a prescription medication in a way not intended by the prescribing doctor**. Prescription drug abuse or problematic use includes everything from taking a friend's prescription painkiller for your backache to snorting or injecting ground-up pills to get high. The prescription <u>drugs most often abused</u> include opioid painkillers, sedatives, anti-anxiety medications and stimulants.

The Symptoms

http://www.mayoclinic.org/diseasesconditions/prescription-drug-abuse/basics/symptoms/con-20032471?reDate=27042017

Poor coordination, anxiety, problems with memory, paranoia, confusion, dizziness, insomnia, slurred speech, unsteady walking, nausea, constipation, reduced appetite, increased pain with higher doses, stealing, forging or selling prescriptions, poor decision making, feeling high, full of energy or sedated, hallucinating, delusional, seeking prescriptions from more than one doctor, taking higher doses than prescribed, continually "losing" prescriptions, so more prescriptions must be written.

Fight

Holy Spirit please pray with me and through me.
Heavenly Father we come to you in the name of
Jesus your son. I ask you to please forgive and
cleanse me from all my sins. Jesus I re-dedicate my
life to you and ask you to be my Savior in every area
of life right now and I know, confess, and believe
with all my heart that you're the Son of God.

Please equip me with the armor you know I will need
to fight against everything that falls under the host
of bondage. Please enable us to operate according to
the rank in your army Jesus you have called us to
and grant us divine, supernatural protection for me,
every one assigned, and related to me from all
demonic counter-attacks.

**Lord God of Heaven, we ask you for forgiveness
for the persons who caused the door to the sins
that caused this bondage to drug addiction, to be
passed down from generation to generation. Lord,
this person was born into this curse, _____ is
innocent. We ask you for a full pardon from this
curse that was imputed into him/her from the
time of conception and ask for total healing &
deliverance please in the name of your Holy Son
Jesus according to John 16:23.**

Lord Jesus, son of the most high God, we ask you to
supply your anointing, glory, and delivering power
upon ___ to destroy the host & god of bondage and
all of their works, powers, influence, spears, barbs,
chains, wires, links, the law of sin, tentacles, claws,
roots, fruits, seeds, their signs ,symptoms, and
manifestations, their effects, adverse effects, stings,
emotions, attacks, wrong mind sets, their

strongholds of poor coordination, anxiety, memory loss, problems with memory, paranoia, confusion, dizziness, insomnia, slurred speech, unsteady walking, nausea, constipation, reduced appetite, increased pain with higher doses, stealing, forging or selling prescriptions, poor decision making, feeling high, full of energy or sedated, hallucinating, delusional, seeking prescriptions from more than one doctor, suicide, taking higher doses than prescribed, continually "losing" prescriptions, so more prescriptions must be written. Jesus please destroy all these things that's come in ___ against____ and in the heavenlies completely.

We ask you Heavenly Father, the Alpha and Omega, to hover your foot over ___ to fully terminate & remove everything that falls under the host of the spirit & god of bondage and their assignments on ___ life without the ability to be re-assigned another specialty. That their banned from the planet earth and all humans, sentenced to the pit of hell until their final place in the lake of fire in the name of Jesus Christ of Nazareth.

Lord Jesus please seal ___ deliverances and this entire prayer in your blood.

Heavenly Father, we ask you for total restoration of every blessing that the devil stole from ____ that he/she doesn't even know about. That this person now lives the abundant life your son Jesus Christ suffered and died for ____ to have immediately please in the name of Jesus Christ of Nazareth we pray and ask for all of these things to be done according to John 16:23 amen.

Bi-Polar

https://psychcentral.com/disorders/bipolar/bipolar-disorder-symptoms/

There are two types of Bi-Polar

- The essential feature of **<u>Bipolar I</u>** is when the person experiences one full manic episode (though the manic episode may have been preceded by and may be followed by hypomanic or major depressive episodes).

- A manic episode is a distinct period during which there is an abnormally, persistently elevated, expansive, or irritable mood and persistently increased activity or energy that is present for most of the day, nearly every day, for a period of at least one week (or any duration if hospitalization is necessary), accompanied by at least three additional symptoms of mania.

- **Bipolar II** requires occurrence (or history) of one or more *Major Depressive Episodes* and at least one *Hypomanic Episode*. Additionally, there has never been a full Manic Episode.

Fight

Holy Spirit please pray with me and through me. Heavenly Father we come to you in the name of Jesus your son. I ask you to please forgive and cleanse me from all my sins. I know you're holy and I ask for your mercy. Jesus I re-dedicate my life to you and ask you to be my Savior in every area of life right now and I know, confess, and believe with all my heart that you're the Son of God.

Please equip me with the armor you know I will need to fight against the generational curse of Bi-polar. Please enable us to operate according to the rank in your army Jesus you have called us to and grant us divine, supernatural protection for me, every one assigned, and related to me from all demonic counter-attacks.

Lord God of Heaven, we ask you for forgiveness for the persons who caused the door to the sins that caused this brain disorder/disease bi-polar, to be passed down from generation to generation. Lord, this person was born into this curse, ____ is innocent. We ask you for a full pardon from this curse that was imputed into him/her from the time of conception & traumatic events that open the door to this disease and ask for total healing & deliverance please in the name of your Holy Son Jesus according to John 16:23.

Father God in Heaven, we lift up _____ right now to you. We ask you Jesus to be our sword of the spirit and supply your anointing, power, and glory to destroy everything that falls under the host & god of infirmity, fear, the dumb and deaf, and bi-polar.

Please terminate every cord, chains, wires, mentally unbalanced attitudes, links, roots, fruits, tentacles, spirits, and all of their signs, symptoms, manifestations, effects, adverse effects, dreams, visions, demonic imaginations, stings, wrong mind sets, emotions, attacks, hypomanic episodes, major depressive episodes, and manic episodes and all that's come in him/her, coming against him/her, and in the heavens completely in the name of Jesus Christ of Nazareth Heavenly Father.

Please deliver & regulate the right levels of brain chemicals [dopamine, serotonin, and norepinephrine] so, they all operate according to your optimum divine design. Restore proper alignment and communication to the brain circuits & neurotransmitters.

We ask you Heavenly Father, the righteous judge, The Alpha and Omega, to hover your foot over ___ to fully terminate & remove every demonic assignments on ___ life without the ability to be re-assigned another specialty. That their banned from the planet earth and all humans, sentenced to the pit of hell until their final place in the lake of fire in the name of Jesus Christ of Nazareth.

Lord Jesus please seal ___ deliverances and this entire prayer in your blood.

Heavenly Father, we ask you for total restoration of every blessing that the devil stole from ____ that he/she doesn't even know about. That this person now lives the abundant life your son Jesus Christ suffered and died for ____ to have immediately please in the name of Jesus Christ of Nazareth we pray and ask for all of these things to be done according to John 16:23 amen.

PTSD

http://www.ptsd.ne.gov/what-is-ptsd.html

PTSD, or Posttraumatic Stress Disorder, is a psychiatric disorder that can occur following the experience or witnessing of a life-threatening events such as military combat, natural disasters, terrorist incidents, serious accidents, or physical or sexual assault in adult or childhood.

Most survivors of trauma return to normal given a little time. However, some people will have stress reactions that do not go away on their own, or may even get worse over time. These individuals may develop PTSD.

People who suffer from PTSD often relive the experience through nightmares and flashbacks, have difficulty sleeping, and feel detached or estranged, and these symptoms can be severe enough and last long enough to significantly impair the person's daily life.

Fight

Holy Spirit please pray with me and through me. Heavenly Father we come to you in the name of Jesus your son. I ask you to please forgive and cleanse me from all my sins. Jesus I re-dedicate my life to you and ask you to be my Savior in every area of life right now and I know, confess, and believe with all my heart that you're the Son of God.

Please equip me with the armor you know I will need to fight against the host of PTSD. Please enable us to operate according to the rank in your army Jesus you have called us to and grant us divine, supernatural protection for me, every one assigned, and related to me from all demonic counter-attacks.

Lord God of Heaven, we ask you for forgiveness for the persons who caused the door to the sins that caused this psychiatric disorder PTSD. Lord, this person contracted this by way of experiencing at some point in their lifetime a life-threatening/traumatic event such as military combat, natural disasters, terrorist incidents, serious accidents, or physical or sexual assault in adult or childhood.
We ask you for a full pardon from this disorder and ask for total healing & deliverance please in the name of your Holy Son Jesus according to John 16:23.

Lord Jesus, son of the most high God, we ask you to bestow your anointing, glory, and power upon ___ to bind & loose everything that falls under the host of the spirit & god of fear and the host of torment.

We ask you Heavenly Father, the Alpha and Omega, to hover your foot over ___ to fully prevent the ability of re-assignment of another demonic specialty.

That their banned from the planet earth and all humans, sentenced to the pit of hell until their final place in the lake of fire in the name of Jesus Christ of Nazareth.

Lord Jesus please seal ___ deliverances and this entire prayer in your blood.

Heavenly Father, we ask you for total restoration of every blessing that the devil stole from ____ that they don't even know about. That this person now lives the abundant life your son Jesus Christ suffered and died for ____ to have immediately please in the name of Jesus Christ of Nazareth we pray and ask for all of these things to be done according to John 16:23 amen.

Anxiety

https://www.psychiatry.org/patients-families/anxiety-disorders/what-are-anxiety-disorders

- Anxiety refers to anticipation of a future concern and is more associated with muscle tension and avoidance behavior.
- **Fear** is an emotional response to an immediate threat and is more associated with a fight or flight reaction – either staying to fight or leaving to escape danger.
- Anxiety disorders can cause people into try to avoid situations that trigger or worsen their symptoms. Job performance, school work, and personal relationships can be affected.

In general, for a person to be diagnosed with an anxiety disorder, the fear or anxiety must:

- Be out of proportion to the situation or age inappropriate.
- Hinder your ability to function normally.

Fight

Holy Spirit please pray with me and through me.
Heavenly Father, we come to you in the name of
Jesus your son and ask you to please forgive and
cleanse me from all my sins. Jesus I re-dedicate my
life to you and ask you to be my Savior in every area
of life right now and I know, confess, and believe
with all my heart that you're the Son of God.

Please equip me with the armor you know I will need
to fight against the host of fear. Please enable us to
operate according to the rank in your army Jesus
you have called us to and grant us divine,
supernatural protection for me, everyone assigned,
and related to me from all demonic counter-attacks.

**Lord God of Heaven, we ask you for forgiveness
for the persons who opened the door to sins that
caused the psychiatric disorder of Anxiety. Lord,
_____ contracted this by way of experiencing a
life-threatening/traumatic event in their adult life
and/or childhood.
We ask you for a full pardon from this disorder
and ask for total healing, restoration of your peace
that surpasses all understanding, & deliverance
please in the name of your Holy Son Jesus
according to John 16:23.**

Lord Jesus, Son of the most high God, we ask you to
bestow your anointing, glory, and power upon ___ to
remove all negative anticipation of future concerns
and enable ____ to loose their body from all muscle
tension and embrace a healthy position in mind,
body, & soul. Please also destroy & annihilate every
trace of avoidance behavior. Impute unto them
righteousness of faith and the courage King David

had when he beat Goliath. When unexpected situations arises kidnap their first mind & all emotional/carnal responses. Let your voice and wisdom be the first they hear Lord.

We ask you Heavenly Father, the righteous judge, the Alpha and Omega, to hover your foot over ___ to fully terminate & remove everything that falls under the host and god of fear & their triggers & assignments on ___ life without the ability to be re-assigned another specialty.
That their banned from the planet earth and all humans, sentenced to the pit of hell until their final place in the lake of fire in the name of Jesus Christ of Nazareth.

Lord Jesus please seal ___ deliverances and this entire prayer in your blood.

Heavenly Father, we ask you for total restoration of every blessing that the devil stole from ___ that they don't even know about. That this person now lives the abundant life your son Jesus Christ suffered and died for ___ to have immediately please in the name of Jesus Christ of Nazareth we pray and ask for all of these things to be done according to John 16:23 amen.

Paranoid Personality Disorder

https://www.psychologytoday.com/blog/hide-and-seek/201205/the-10-personality-disorders

<u>Cluster A</u> comprises paranoid, schizoid, and schizotypal personality disorders.

- Paranoid personality disorder is characterized by a pervasive distrust of others, including even friends, family, and partner. As a result, the person is guarded and suspicious, and constantly on the lookout for clues or suggestions to validate his fears.

- He also has a strong sense of personal rights: **he/she is overly sensitive** to setbacks and rebuffs, easily feels shame and humiliation, and persistently bears grudges.
  Unsurprisingly, he tends to withdraw from others and to struggle with building close relationships.

- The principal ego defense in paranoid PD is projection, which involves attributing one's unacceptable thoughts and feelings to other people. A large long-term twin study found that paranoid PD is modestly heritable, and that it shares a portion of its genetic and environmental risk factors with schizoid PD and schizotypal PD.

Fight

Holy Spirit please pray with me and through me. Heavenly Father we come to you in the name of Jesus your son. I ask you to please forgive and cleanse me from all my sins. Jesus I re-dedicate my life to you and ask you to be my Savior in every area of life right now and I know, confess, and believe with all my heart that you're the Son of God.

Please equip me with the armor you know I will need to fight against the host & god of fear and rejection. Please enable us to operate according to the rank in your army Jesus you have called us to and grant us divine, supernatural protection for me, every one assigned, and related to me from all demonic counter-attacks.

Lord God of Heaven, we ask you for forgiveness for the persons who caused the door to the sins that caused this generational curse and disorder of paranoia. Lord, this person was born into this curse/disorder ___ is innocent. We ask you for a full pardon from this curse that was imputed into him/her from the time of conception and ask for total healing & deliverance please in the name of your Holy Son Jesus according to John 16:23.

Lord Jesus, son of the most high God, we ask you to bestow your anointing, glory, and power upon ___ to deliver ___ from all the characteristics of paranoid personality disorder. Demolish all of their chains, links, tentacles, spears, barbs, wires, roots, fruits, signs, symptoms, manifestations, effects, adverse effects, stings, wrong mind sets, emotional attacks, coming in, on, against and through ___ .

We ask you Heavenly Father, the most high God, the Alpha and Omega, to hover your foot over ___ to fully terminate & remove everything that falls under the host of the god of fear and rejection & their assignments on ___ life without the ability to be re-assigned another specialty.

That their banned from the planet earth and all humans, sentenced to the pit of hell until their final place in the lake of fire in the name of Jesus Christ of Nazareth.

Lord Jesus please seal ___ deliverances and this entire prayer in your blood.

Heavenly Father, we ask you for total restoration of every blessing that the devil stole from ___ that they don't even know about. That this person now lives the abundant life your son Jesus Christ suffered and died for ___ to have immediately please in the name of Jesus Christ of Nazareth we pray and ask for all of these things to be done according to John 16:23 amen.

Schizoid Personality Disorder

https://www.psychologytoday.com/blog/hide-and-seek/201205/the-10-personality-disorders

- The term 'schizoid' designates a natural tendency to direct attention toward one's inner life and away from the external world.

- A person with schizoid PD is **detached** and aloof and prone to introspection and fantasy.

- He has no desire for social or sexual relationships, is indifferent to others and to social norms and conventions, and lacks emotional response.

- A competing theory about people with schizoid PD is that they are in fact highly sensitive with a rich inner life: they experience a deep longing for intimacy but find initiating and maintaining close relationships too difficult or distressing, and so retreat into their inner world.

- People with schizoid PD rarely present to medical attention because, despite their reluctance to form close relationships, they are generally well functioning, and quite untroubled by their apparent oddness.

Fight

Holy Spirit please pray with me and through me. Heavenly Father we come to you in the name of Jesus your son. I ask you to please forgive and cleanse me from all my sins. Jesus I re-dedicate my life to you and ask you to be my Savior in every area of life right now and I know, confess, and believe with all my heart that you're the Son of God.

Please equip me with the armor you know I will need to fight against the hosts of leviathan and the gods of divination. Please enable us to operate according to the rank in your army Jesus you have called us to and grant us divine, supernatural protection for me, every one assigned, and related to me from all demonic counter-attacks.

Lord God of Heaven, we ask you for forgiveness for the persons who opened the door to the sins that caused this personality disorder, to be passed down or transferred. Lord, this person was born into this ____ is innocent. We ask you for a full pardon from this disorder that was imputed into him/her from the time of conception even until now and ask for total healing & deliverance please in the name of your Holy Son Jesus according to John 16:23.

Lord Jesus, son of the most high God, we ask you to supply your anointing, glory, and power upon ___ to supernaturally deliver _____ from every demonic vicious cycle, lack of having emotional responses & living in a fantasy world, the negative concepts of initiating and maintaining close relationships being too difficult or distressing,

We ask you Heavenly Father, the righteous judge, the Alpha and Omega, to hover your foot over ___ to fully terminate & remove everything that falls under the host of leviathan & the gods of divination and their assignments on ___ life without the ability to be re-assigned another specialty.
That their banned from the planet earth and all humans, sentenced to the pit of hell until their final place in the lake of fire in the name of Jesus Christ of Nazareth.

Lord Jesus please seal ___ deliverances and this entire prayer in your blood.

Heavenly Father, we ask you to restore every blessing that the devil stole from ____ that they don't even know about, every blessing, heavenly relationship, **fresh fire of rejuvenation for life**, favor, prosperity, **righteous desire for healthy friendships & relationship, having their deep longing for intimacy fulfilled in a Godly-productive manner,** clarity and focus in the mind, sharp attention to detail, the spirit of a finisher, the spirit of a winner, the heart of a servant, true humility, integrity, honesty, loyalty only to good things in the mind of ____ , every promise written in the Bible, and the abundant life your son Jesus Christ suffered and died for ____ to have right now please in the name of Jesus Christ of Nazareth we pray and ask for all of these things to be done according to John 16:23 amen.

Schizotypal Disorder

https://www.psychologytoday.com/blog/hide-and-seek/201205/the-10-personality-disorders

- Schizotypal PD is characterized by oddities of appearance, behavior, and speech, unusual perceptual experiences, and anomalies of thinking similar to those seen in schizophrenia.
- These latter can include odd beliefs, magical thinking (for instance, thinking that speaking of the devil can make him appear), suspiciousness, and obsessive ruminations.
- People with schizotypal PD **often fear social interaction and think of others as harmful**. This may lead them to develop so-called ideas of reference, that is, beliefs or intuitions that events and happenings are somehow related to them.
- So whereas people with schizotypal PD and people with schizoid PD both avoid social interaction, with the former it is because they fear others, whereas with the latter it is because they have no desire to interact with others or find interacting with others too difficult.
- People with schizotypal PD have a higher than average probability of developing schizophrenia, and the condition used to be called 'latent schizophrenia'.

Fight

Holy Spirit please pray with me and through me. Heavenly Father we come to you in the name of Jesus your son. I ask you to please forgive and cleanse me from all my sins. Jesus I re-dedicate my life to you and ask you to be my Savior in every area of life right now and I know, confess, and believe with all my heart that you're the Son of God.

Please equip me with the armor you know I will need to fight against everything that falls under the hosts of legion. Please enable us to operate according to the rank in your army Jesus you have called us to and grant us divine, supernatural protection for me, every one assigned, and related to me from all demonic counter-attacks.

Lord God of Heaven, we ask you for forgiveness for the persons who opened the door to the sins & hazardous life situations that caused this personality disorder, schizotypal, to kidnap _____ total existence.

Lord, on behalf of _____ in the name of your Holy son Jesus, we ask you for a full pardon from this disorder that was imputed into him/her. Lord Jesus please supply your healing & deliverance anointing to save _____ please Heavenly Father in the name of your Holy Son Jesus according to John 14:13-14.

Lord Jesus, son of the most high God, we ask you to bestow your anointing, glory, and power upon ___ to deliver him/ her from negative characteristics of delusion, self-deception, lies of the enemy, the law of sin, self-destruction, hearing from demons, seeing demons and devils, odd beliefs, magical thinking, suspiciousness, obsessive ruminations & the fear of social interaction and thinking of all others as harmful.

We ask you Heavenly Father, the Alpha and Omega, to hover your foot over ___ to fully terminate & remove everything that falls under the host of legion, the gods of deception, and the gods of seducing spirits, their vicious circles & their assignments on ___ life without the ability to be re-assigned another specialty.

That their banned from the planet earth and all humans, sentenced to the pit of hell until their final place in the lake of fire in the name of Jesus Christ of Nazareth.

Lord Jesus please seal ___ deliverances and this entire prayer in your blood.

Heavenly Father, we ask you for total restoration of every blessing that the devil stole from ____ that they don't even know about. That this person now lives the abundant life your son Jesus Christ suffered and died for ____ to have immediately please in the name of Jesus Christ of Nazareth we pray and ask for all of these things to be done according to John 16:23 amen.

Antisocial Personality Disorder

https://www.psychologytoday.com/blog/hide-and-seek/201205/the-10-personality-disorders

Cluster B comprises antisocial, borderline, histrionic, and narcissistic personality disorders. Antisocial PD is much more common in men than in women, and is **characterized by a callous unconcern for the feelings of others.**

- The person disregards social rules and obligations, is irritable and aggressive, acts impulsively, lacks guilt, and fails to learn from experience.
- In many cases, he has no difficulty finding relationships—and can even appear superficially charming (the so-called 'charming psychopath')—but these relationships are usually fiery, turbulent, and short-lived.
- As antisocial PD is the mental disorder most closely correlated with crime, he is likely to have a criminal record or a history of being in and out of prison.

Fight

Holy Spirit please pray with me and through me.
Heavenly Father we come to you in the name of
Jesus your son. I ask you to please forgive and
cleanse me from all my sins. Jesus I re-dedicate my
life to you and ask you to be my Savior in every area
of life right now and I know, confess, and believe
with all my heart that you're the Son of God.

Please equip me with the armor you know I will need
to fight against everything that falls under the hosts
& gods of fear, anger, and rejection. Please enable us
to operate according to the rank in your army Jesus
you have called us to and grant us divine,
supernatural protection for me, every one assigned,
and related to me from all demonic counter-attacks.

**Lord God of Heaven, we ask you for forgiveness
for the persons who opened the door to the sins &
hazardous life situations that caused this
personality disorder to kidnap _____ entire
existence.**

**Lord, on behalf of _____ in the name of your Holy
son Jesus, we ask you for a full pardon from this
disorder that was imputed into him/her. Lord
Jesus please supply your healing, deliverance, &
anointing to save _____ from this disorder
please. Heavenly Father, we ask you to do all of
this in the name of your Holy Son Jesus according
to John 14:13-14.**

Lord Jesus, son of the most high God, we ask you to
bestow your anointing, glory, and power upon ___ to
impart compassion for others as you have, to have
the upmost respect and obedience for social rules

and obligations, is no longer bound to irritability &
being aggressive, thinks about consequences long
and hard before making a decision, from now on
makes healthy and good decisions, please impart
strong moral convictions, that he/she truly asks for
forgiveness and understands why, no longer repeats
the same offenses, learns from his/her mistakes, no
longer commits crime and stays out of prison,
mental wards, rehab centers, and delinquent
centers, and juvenile homes.

**We ask you Heavenly Father, to hover your foot
over ____ to fully terminate & remove everything
falls under the hosts & gods of fear, anger, and
rejection assignments on ____ life without the
ability to be re-assigned another specialty.**

That their banned from the planet earth and all
humans, sentenced to the pit of hell until their final
place in the lake of fire in the name of Jesus Christ
of Nazareth.

Lord Jesus please seal ___ deliverances and this
entire prayer in your blood.

Heavenly Father, we ask you for total restoration of
every blessing that the devil stole from ____ that they
don't even know about. That this person now lives
the abundant life your son Jesus Christ suffered
and died for ____ to have right now please in the
name of Jesus Christ of Nazareth we pray and ask
for all of these things to be done according to John
16:23 amen.

Borderline Personality Disorder

https://www.psychologytoday.com/blog/hide-and-seek/201205/the-10-personality-disorders

- In borderline PD (or emotionally unstable PD), the person essentially **lacks a sense of self, and, as a result, experiences feelings of emptiness and fears of abandonment.**

- There is a pattern of intense but unstable relationships, emotional instability, outbursts of anger and violence (especially in response to criticism), and impulsive behavior.

- Suicidal threats and acts of self-harm are common, for which reason many people with borderline PD frequently come to medical attention.

- Borderline PD was so called because it was thought to lie on the 'borderline' **between neurotic (anxiety) disorders and psychotic disorders such as schizophrenia and bipolar disorder.**

- It has been suggested that borderline personality disorder often results from *childhood sexual abuse*, and that it is more common in women in part because women are more likely to suffer sexual abuse.

Fight

Holy Spirit please pray with me and through me.
Heavenly Father we come to you in the name of
Jesus your son. I ask you to please forgive and
cleanse me from all my sins. Jesus I re-dedicate my
life to you and ask you to be my Savior in every area
of life right now and I know, confess, and believe
with all my heart that you're the Son of God. Please
equip me with the armor you know I will need to
fight against the borderline personality disorder.
Please enable us to operate according to the rank in
your army Jesus you have called us to and grant us
divine, supernatural protection for me, every one
assigned, and related to me from all demonic
counter-attacks.

**Lord God of Heaven, we ask you for forgiveness
for the persons who opened the door to the sins &
hazardous life situations that caused this
borderline personality disorder to kidnap _____
entire existence. Lord, on behalf of _____ in the
name of your Holy son Jesus, we ask you for a full
pardon from this disorder that was imputed into
him/her.**

Lord Jesus, son of the most high God, we ask you to
supply your anointing, glory, and delivering power
upon ___ to destroy everything that falls under the
hosts & gods of perverse, anti-christs, fear, rape,
molestation, murder and the entire demonic
kingdom of jezebel & ahab and all of their works,
powers, influence, spears, barbs, chains, wires,
links, the law of sin, tentacles, claws, roots, fruits,
seeds planted and , their embedded signs,
symptoms, and manifestations, their effects, adverse
effects, stings, emotions, attacks, wrong mind sets,

53

their strongholds of anxiety, memory loss, bitterness, the poison of bitterness, un-forgiveness, paranoia, insomnia, poor decision making, suicide, self-destruction, lack of self-worth and respect, emptiness, fear of abandonment, unstable relationships, emotional instability, outbursts of anger and violence (especially in response to criticism), and impulsive & neurotic behaviors. Jesus please destroy all these things that's come in ___ against___ and everyone that's assigned and related to them completely.

We ask you Heavenly Father, to hover your foot over ___ to fully terminate & remove everything that came against ___ due to a demonic assignment since birth to destroy this person's life and that you shut the door forever without the ability to be re-assigned another specialty. That their banned from the planet earth and all humans, sentenced to the pit of hell until their final place in the lake of fire in the name of Jesus Christ of Nazareth.

Lord Jesus please seal ___ deliverances and this entire prayer in the power of your blood.

Heavenly Father, we ask you for total restoration of every blessing that the devil stole from ___ that they don't even know about. That this person now lives the abundant life your son Jesus Christ suffered and died for ___ to have immediately please in the name of Jesus Christ of Nazareth we pray and ask for all of these things to be done according to John 16:23 amen.

Histrionic Personality Disorder

https://www.psychologytoday.com/blog/hide-and-seek/201205/the-10-personality-disorders

People with histrionic PD **lack a sense of self-worth, and depend for their wellbeing on attracting the attention and approval of others.**

They often seem to be dramatizing or 'playing a part' in a bid to be heard and seen. Indeed, 'histrionic' derives from the Latin *histrionicus*, 'pertaining to the actor'.

People with histrionic PD may take great care of their appearance and behave in a manner that is overly charming or inappropriately seductive.

As they crave excitement and act on impulse or suggestion, they can place themselves at risk of accident or exploitation. Their dealings with others often seem insincere or superficial, which, in the longer term, can adversely impact on their social and romantic relationships.

This is especially distressing to them, as they are sensitive **to criticism and rejection, and react badly to loss or failure.**

A vicious circle may take hold in which the more rejected they feel, the more histrionic they become; and the more histrionic they become, the more rejected they feel. It can be argued that *a vicious circle* of some kind is at the heart of every personality disorder, and, indeed, every mental disorder.

Fight

Holy Spirit please pray with me and through me.
Heavenly Father we come to you in the name of
Jesus your son. I ask you to please forgive and
cleanse me from all my sins. Jesus I re-dedicate my
life to you and ask you to be my Savior in every area
of life right now and I know, confess, and believe
with all my heart that you're the Son of God.

Please equip me with the armor you know I will need
to fight against the personality disorder of histrionic.
Please enable us to operate according to the rank in
your army Jesus you have called us to and grant us
divine, supernatural protection for me, every one
assigned, and related to me from all demonic
counter-attacks.

**Lord God of Heaven, we ask you for forgiveness
for the persons who opened the door to the sins &
hazardous life situations that caused this
histrionic personality disorder to kidnap _____
entire existence. Lord, on behalf of _____ in the
name of your Holy son Jesus, we ask you for a full
pardon from this disorder that was imputed or
transferred into him/her in every which way.**

Lord Jesus, son of the most high God, we ask you to
supply your anointing, glory, and delivering power
upon ___ to destroy everything that falls under the
hosts & gods of all perversions, anti-christs, lucifer,
adultery, seduction, murder, incubus & succubus,
rejection, & pornography and all of their works,
powers, influence, spears, barbs, works of the flesh,
chains, wires, links, the law of sin, tentacles, claws,
roots, fruits, seeds planted and , their embedded

signs, symptoms, and manifestations, their effects, adverse effects, stings, emotions, attacks, wrong mind sets & their strongholds of lacking a sense of self-worth, and dependence on their wellbeing for attracting the attention and approval of others, behaving in a desperate manner that is overly charming or inappropriately seductive to gain attention, irrational actions committed on impulse or suggestions, that place them at risk of accident or exploitation.

Lord, also deliver _____ from inconsiderate dealings with others which, in the longer term, can adversely impact on their social and romantic relationships & _____ carnal and immature reactions to loss, failure, criticism, and rejection.

Jesus, thou son of David, supply your power to destroy the chains of the vicious circle in which the more _____ faces rejection, the more histrionic he/she becomes; and the more histrionic he/she becomes, the more rejected ___ feel.

We ask you Heavenly Father, to hover your foot over ___ to fully terminate & remove everything that came against _____ due to a demonic assignment since birth to destroy this person's life and that you shut the door forever without the ability to be re-assigned another specialty. That their banned from the planet earth and all humans, sentenced to the pit of hell until their final place in the lake of fire in the name of Jesus Christ of Nazareth.

Lord Jesus please seal ___ deliverances and this entire prayer in the power of your blood.

Heavenly Father, we ask you for total restoration of every blessing that the devil stole from _____ that _____ doesn't even know about. That this person now lives the abundant life your son Jesus Christ suffered and died for _____ to have immediately please in the name of Jesus Christ of Nazareth we pray and ask for all of these things to be done according to John 16:23 amen.

Narcissistic Personality Disorder

https://www.psychologytoday.com/blog/hide-and-seek/201205/the-10-personality-disorders

- In narcissistic PD, **the person has an extreme feeling of self-importance, a sense of entitlement, and a need to be admired.**
- He/She is envious of others and expects them to be the same of him.
- He/She lacks empathy and readily lies and exploits others to achieve his aims.
- To others, he may seem self-absorbed, controlling, intolerant, selfish, or insensitive. If he feels obstructed or ridiculed, he can fly into a fit of destructive anger and revenge. Such a reaction is sometimes called 'narcissistic rage', and can have disastrous consequences for all those involved.

Fight

Holy Spirit please pray with me and through me. Heavenly Father we come to you in the name of Jesus your son. I ask you to please forgive and cleanse me from all my sins. Jesus I re-dedicate my life to you and ask you to be my Savior in every area of life right now and I know, confess, and believe with all my heart that you're the Son of God.

Please equip me with the armor you know I will need to fight against the narcissistic personality disorder. Please enable us to operate according to the rank in your army Jesus you have called us to and grant us divine, supernatural protection for me, every one assigned, and related to me from all demonic counter-attacks.

Lord God of Heaven, we ask you for forgiveness for the persons who opened the door to the sins & hazardous life situations that caused this narcissistic personality disorder to kidnap _____ entire existence. Lord, on behalf of _____ in the name of your Holy son Jesus, we ask you for a full pardon from this disorder that was imputed or transferred into him/her in every which way.

Lord Jesus, son of the most high God, we ask you to supply your anointing, glory, and delivering power upon ___ to destroy everything that falls under the hosts & gods of anger, anti-christs, lucifer, satan, pride, rebellion, witchcraft, saul, balaam, baal, jezebel & ahab and their entire kingdom, jealousy, vanity, error, death, and all of their works, powers, influence, spears, barbs, works of the flesh, chains, wires, links, the law of sin, tentacles, claws, roots, fruits, seeds planted and , their embedded signs, symptoms, and manifestations, their effects, adverse effects, stings, emotions, attacks, wrong mind sets & their strongholds of having an extreme feeling of self-importance, a sense of entitlement, and a need to be admired, becoming envious of others and expects them to be the same of him/her, lacking true empathy and readily lies and exploits others to achieve his/her objectives, being obsessively self-absorbed, controlling, contentious, intolerant, selfish, insensitive, revengeful, destructive to self and others, and having temper-tantrums when doesn't get own way, when feeling ridiculed, and rejected.

We ask you Heavenly Father, to hover your foot over ___ to fully terminate & remove the vicious cycle and circle of this disorder and everything that falls under it since birth to destroy this person's life. Please shut this door forever without the ability to be re-assigned another specialty. That this entity is banned from the planet earth and all humans, sentenced to the pit of hell until their final place in the lake of fire in the name of Jesus Christ of Nazareth.

Lord Jesus please seal ___ deliverances and this entire prayer in the power of your blood.

Heavenly Father, we ask you for total restoration of every blessing that the devil stole from ___ that ___ doesn't even know about. That this person now lives the abundant life your son Jesus Christ suffered and died for ___ to have immediately please in the name of Jesus Christ of Nazareth we pray and ask for all of these things to be done according to John 16:23 amen.

Avoidant Personality Disorder

https://www.psychologytoday.com/blog/hide-and-seek/201205/the-10-personality-disorders

Cluster C comprises avoidant, dependent, and anankastic personality disorders.

People with avoidant PD **believe that they are socially inept, unappealing, or inferior, and constantly fear being embarrassed, criticized, or rejected.** They avoid meeting others unless they are certain of being liked, and are restrained even in their intimate relationships.

Avoidant PD is **strongly associated with anxiety disorders**, and may also be associated with actual or felt rejection by parents or peers in childhood.

Research suggests that people with avoidant PD excessively monitor internal reactions, both their own and those of others, which prevents them from engaging naturally or fluently in social situations.

A vicious circle takes hold in which the more they monitor their internal reactions, the more inept they feel; and the more inept they feel, the more they monitor their internal reactions.

Fight

Holy Spirit please pray with me and through me. Heavenly Father we come to you in the name of Jesus your son. I ask you to please forgive and cleanse me from all my sins. Jesus I re-dedicate my life to you and ask you to be my Savior in every area of life right now and I know, confess, and believe with all my heart that you're the Son of God.

Please equip me with the armor you know I will need to fight against the Avoidant Personality Disorder. Please enable us to operate according to the rank in your army Jesus you have called us to and grant us divine, supernatural protection for me, every one assigned, and related to me from all demonic counter-attacks.

Lord God of Heaven, we ask you for forgiveness for the persons who opened the door to the sins & hazardous life situations that caused this avoidant personality disorder to kidnap _____ entire existence. Lord, on behalf of _____ in the name of your Holy son Jesus, we ask you for a full pardon from this disorder that was imputed or transferred into him/her in every which way.

Lord Jesus, son of the most high God, we ask you to supply your anointing, glory, and delivering power upon ___ to destroy everything that falls under the hosts & gods of fear, error, & rejection, their vicious circles & cycles, and all of their works, powers, influence, spears, barbs, works of the flesh, chains, wires, links, the law of sin, tentacles, claws, roots, fruits, seeds planted and , their embedded signs, symptoms, and manifestations, their effects, adverse effects, stings, emotions, attacks, wrong mind sets & their strongholds of believing that he/she are socially inept, unappealing, or inferior, and constantly in fear of being embarrassed, criticized, or rejected. Relational strongholds associated with the spirit of anxiety, the inability to engage naturally in social environments, and lastly, the internal vicious circle causing he/she to monitor their internal reactions & diagnosis.

We ask you Heavenly Father, to hover your foot over ___ to fully terminate & remove the demonic assignments that came against ____ at the time of conception to destroy this person's life. Please shut and seal those doors forever. Everything that's leaving ___ cannot be re-assigned another specialty. That their banned from the planet earth and all humans, sentenced to the pit of hell until their final place in the lake of fire in the name of Jesus Christ of Nazareth.

Lord Jesus please seal ___ deliverances and this entire prayer in the power of your blood.

Heavenly Father, we ask you for total restoration of every blessing that the devil stole from ____ that ____ doesn't even know about. That this person now lives the abundant life your son Jesus Christ suffered and died for ____ to have immediately please in the name of Jesus Christ of Nazareth we pray and ask for all of these things to be done according to John 16:23 amen.

Dependent Personality Disorder

https://www.psychologytoday.com/blog/hide-and-
seek/201205/the-10-personality-disorders

Dependent PD is characterized **by a lack of self-
confidence and an excessive need to be looked
after**.

The person needs a lot of help in making
everyday decisions and surrenders important life
decisions to the care of others. He greatly fears
abandonment and may go through considerable
lengths to secure and maintain relationships.

A person with dependent PD sees himself as
inadequate and helpless, and so surrenders
personal responsibility and submits himself to
one or more protective others.

He imagines that he is at one with these
protective other(s), whom he idealizes as
competent and powerful, and towards whom he
behaves in a manner that is ingratiating and self-
effacing.

People with dependent PD often end up with
people with a cluster B personality disorder, who
feed on the unconditional high regard in which
they are held.

Overall, **people with dependent PD maintain a
naïve and child-like perspective, and have**

limited insight into themselves and others. This entrenches their dependency, and leaves them vulnerable to abuse and exploitation.

Fight

Holy Spirit please pray with me and through me. Heavenly Father we come to you in the name of Jesus your son. I ask you to please forgive and cleanse me from all my sins. Jesus I re-dedicate my life to you and ask you to be my Savior in every area of life right now and I know, confess, and believe with all my heart that you're the Son of God.

Please equip me with the armor you know I will need to fight against dependent personality disorder. Please enable us to operate according to the rank in your army Jesus you have called us to and grant us divine, supernatural protection for me, every one assigned, and related to me from all demonic counter-attacks.

Lord God of Heaven, we ask you for forgiveness for the persons who opened the door to the sins & hazardous life situations that caused this dependent personality disorder to kidnap _____ entire existence. Lord, on behalf of _____ in the name of your Holy son Jesus, we ask you for a full pardon from this disorder that was imputed or transferred into him/her in every which way.

Lord Jesus, son of the most high God, we ask you to supply your anointing, glory, and delivering power upon ___ to destroy everything that falls under the hosts & gods of fear, error, neglect, & rejection, their vicious circles & cycles, and all of their works, powers, influence, spears, barbs, works of the flesh, chains, wires, links, the law of sin, tentacles, claws, roots, fruits, seeds planted and , their embedded signs, symptoms, and manifestations, their effects, adverse effects, stings, emotions, attacks, wrong mind sets & their strongholds of all the characteristics that are associated & define this disorder.

We ask you Heavenly Father, to hover your foot over ___ to fully terminate & remove the demonic assignments that came against ____ at the time of conception to destroy this person's life. Please shut and seal those doors forever. Everything that's leaving ___ cannot be re-assigned another specialty. Their banned from the planet earth and all humans, sentenced to the pit of hell until their final place in the lake of fire in the name of Jesus Christ of Nazareth.

Lord Jesus please seal ___ deliverances and this entire prayer in the power of your blood.

Heavenly Father, we ask you for total restoration of every blessing that the devil stole from ____ that ____ doesn't even know about. That this person now lives the abundant life your son Jesus Christ suffered and died for _____ to have immediately please in the name of Jesus Christ of Nazareth we pray and ask for all of these things to be done according to John 16:23 amen.

Anankastic Personality Disorder

https://www.psychologytoday.com/blog/hide-and-seek/201205/the-10-personality-disorders

Anankastic PD is characterized by **excessive preoccupation with details, rules, lists, order, organization, or schedules; perfectionism so extreme that it prevents a task from being completed; and devotion to work and productivity at the expense of leisure and relationships.**

A person with anankastic PD is typically doubting and cautious, rigid and controlling, humorless, and miserly.

His/Her underlying anxiety arises from a perceived **lack of control over a world that eludes his understanding; and the more he tries to exert control, the more out of control he feels.**

In consequence, he has little tolerance for complexity or nuance, and tends to simplify the world by seeing things as either all good or all bad.

His relationships with colleagues, friends, and family are often strained by the unreasonable and inflexible demands that he makes upon them.

Fight

Holy Spirit please pray with me and through me. Heavenly Father we come to you in the name of Jesus your son. I ask you to please forgive and cleanse me from all my sins. Jesus I re-dedicate my life to you and ask you to be my Savior in every area of life right now and I know, confess, and believe with all my heart that you're the Son of God.

Please equip me with the armor you know I will need to fight against anankastic personality disorder. Please enable us to operate according to the rank in your army Jesus you have called us to and grant us divine, supernatural protection for me, every one assigned, and related to me from all demonic counter-attacks.

Lord God of Heaven, we ask you for forgiveness for the persons who opened the door to the sins & hazardous life situations that caused this anankastic personality disorder to kidnap _____ entire existence. Lord, on behalf of _____ in the name of your Holy son Jesus, we ask you for a full pardon from this disorder that was imputed or transferred into him/her in every which way.

Lord Jesus, son of the most high God, we ask you to supply your anointing, glory, and delivering power upon ___ to destroy everything that falls under the hosts & gods of jezebel and ahab & their entire kingdom, fear, control, and vanity their vicious circles & cycles, and all of their works, powers, influence, spears, barbs, works of the flesh, chains, wires, links, the law of sin, tentacles, claws, roots, fruits, seeds planted and , their embedded signs, symptoms, and manifestations, their effects, adverse effects, stings, emotions, attacks, wrong mind sets & their strongholds of all the characteristics & traits that are define and connected to this disorder.

We ask you Heavenly Father, to hover your foot over ___ to fully terminate & remove the demonic assignments that came against ____ at the time of conception to destroy this person's life. Please shut and seal those doors forever. Everything that's leaving ___ cannot be re-assigned another specialty. Their banned from the planet earth and all humans, sentenced to the pit of hell until their final place in the lake of fire in the name of Jesus Christ of Nazareth.

Lord Jesus please seal ___ deliverances and this entire prayer in the power of your blood.

Heavenly Father, we ask you for total restoration of every blessing that the devil stole from ____ that ____ doesn't even know about. That this person now lives the abundant life your son Jesus Christ suffered and died for _____ to have immediately please in the name of Jesus Christ of Nazareth we pray and ask for all of these things to be done according to John 16:23 amen.

Heart Attack

http://www.mayoclinic.org/diseases-conditions/heart-attack/basics/definition/con-20019520

According to the Mayo clinic staff, a heart attack occurs when the flow of blood to the heart is blocked, most often by a build-up of fat, cholesterol and other substances, which form a plaque in the arteries that feed the heart (coronary arteries).

The interrupted blood flow can damage or destroy part of the heart muscle.
A heart attack, also called a *myocardial infarction*, can be fatal, but treatment has improved dramatically over the years.

Fight

Holy Spirit please pray with me and through me. Heavenly Father we come to you in the name of Jesus your son. I ask you to please forgive and cleanse me from all my sins. Jesus I re-dedicate my life to you and ask you to be my Savior in every area of life right now and I know, confess, and believe with all my heart that you're the Son of God.

Please equip me with the armor you know I will need to fight against the spirit of heart attack. Please enable us to operate according to the rank in your army Jesus you have called us to and grant us divine, supernatural protection for me, every one assigned, and related to me from all demonic counter-attacks.

Lord God of Heaven, we ask you for forgiveness for the persons who caused the door to the sins that caused this heart attack illness, to be passed down from generation to generation. Lord, this person was born into this curse, ____ is innocent. We ask you for a full pardon from this curse that was imputed into him/her from the time of conception and ask for total healing & deliverance please in the name of your Holy Son Jesus according to John 16:23.

Lord Jesus, son of the most high God, we ask you to bestow your anointing, glory, and power upon ___ to deliver him/her from everything that falls under the host & god of premature death and murder. Please remove all obstructions and plaque immediately out of the pathway of proper blood flow leading to the heart. We ask you to rebuke all forms of interrupted blood flow from ___ system and enable him/her to make the necessary healthy changes to live a better life and complete the assignment you have for them.

We ask you Heavenly Father, to hover your foot over ___ to fully terminate & remove the demonic assignments that came against ____ at the time of conception to destroy this person's life. Please shut and seal those doors forever. Everything that's leaving ___ cannot be re-assigned another specialty. Their banned from the planet earth and all humans, sentenced to the pit of hell until their final place in the lake of fire in the name of Jesus Christ of Nazareth.

Lord Jesus please seal ___ deliverances and this entire prayer in the power of your blood.

Heavenly Father, we ask you for total restoration of every blessing that the devil stole from ____ that ____ doesn't even know about. That this person now lives the abundant life your son Jesus Christ suffered and died for _____ to have immediately please in the name of Jesus Christ of Nazareth we pray and ask for all of these things to be done according to John 16:23 amen.

Diabetes

http://www.webmd.com/diabetes/understanding-diabetes-basics#1

According to WebMD, Diabetes is the most common disorder of the endocrine (hormone) system, occurs when blood sugar levels in the body consistently stay above normal.

Diabetes is a disease brought on by either the body's inability to make insulin (type 1 diabetes) or by the body not responding to the effects of insulin (type 2 diabetes).

Insulin is one of the main hormones that regulates blood sugar levels and allows the body to use sugar (called glucose) for energy.

Impaired glucose tolerance is known as pre-diabetes.

Fight

Holy Spirit please pray with me and through me. Heavenly Father we come to you in the name of Jesus your son. I ask you to please forgive and cleanse me from all my sins. Jesus I re-dedicate my life to you and ask you to be my Savior in every area of life right now and I know, confess, and believe with all my heart that you're the Son of God.

Please equip me with the armor you know I will need to fight against the generational curse of diabetes. Please enable us to operate according to the rank in your army Jesus you have called us to and grant us divine, supernatural protection for me, every one assigned, and related to me from all demonic counter-attacks.

Lord God of Heaven, we ask you for forgiveness for the persons who caused the door to the sins that caused the illness of diabetes, to be passed down from generation to generation. Lord, this person was born into this curse, ____ is innocent. We ask you for a full pardon from this curse that was imputed into him/her from the time of conception and ask for total healing & deliverance please in the name of your Holy Son Jesus according to John 16:23.

Lord Jesus, son of the most high God, we ask you to bestow your healing anointing, glory, and power upon ___ to regulate the blood sugar levels to a normal balance of functioning. Lord please enable the organ to effectively produce insulin and the body become receptive to respond to the effects of insulin according to your optimum divine design. Please rebuke all impaired glucose tolerance.

We ask you Heavenly Father, to hover your foot over ___ to fully terminate & remove the demonic assignments that came against ____ at the time of conception to destroy this person's life. Please shut and seal those doors forever. Everything that's leaving ___ cannot be re-assigned another specialty. Their banned from the planet earth and all humans, sentenced to the pit of hell until their final place in the lake of fire in the name of Jesus Christ of Nazareth.

Lord Jesus please seal ___ deliverances and this entire prayer in the power of your blood.

Heavenly Father, we ask you for total restoration of every blessing that the devil stole from ____ that ____ doesn't even know about. That this person now lives the abundant life your son Jesus Christ suffered and died for ____ to have immediately please in the name of Jesus Christ of Nazareth we pray and ask for all of these things to be done according to John 16:23 amen.

Obesity

https://www.nature.com/articles/srep34122

In a study conducted by Dirk De Ridder, Patrick Manning, Sook Ling Leong, Samantha Ross, Wayne Sutherland, Caroline Horwath & Sven Vanneste **brain activity** in food-addicted and non-food-addicted obese people was compared to alcohol-addicted and non-addicted lean controls.

The results displayed showed that food addiction shares common **neural brain activity** with alcohol addiction.

Target specific pathophysiologic abnormalities.

Homeostatic control centers in the functions of the brain plays a pivotal role in body weight regulation.

The clinical similarities has led to the idea that obesity and alcohol addiction may share common *molecular, cellular and systems-level mechanisms.*

The Taq1A minor (A1) allele of the dopamine receptor D2 **(DRD2) gene**, which has been associated with alcoholism; substance-misuse disorders, including cocaine, smoking and opioid dependence and obesity.

Fight

Holy Spirit please pray with me and through me.
Heavenly Father we come to you in the name of
Jesus your son. I ask you to please forgive and
cleanse me from all my sins. Jesus I re-dedicate my
life to you and ask you to be my Savior in every area
of life right now and I know, confess, and believe
with all my heart that you're the Son of God.

Please equip me with the armor you know I will need
to fight against the generational curse of obesity.
Please enable us to operate according to the rank in
your army Jesus you have called us to and grant us
divine, supernatural protection for me, every one
assigned, and related to me from all demonic
counter-attacks.

**Lord God of Heaven, we ask you for forgiveness
for the persons who caused the door to the sins
that caused the disease of obesity, to be passed
down from generation to generation.**

**We also ask you Lord, on behalf of this person, to
dismantle the negative effects from life situations
to cause ____ to use food as a coping mechanism
for self-healing.**

**We ask you for a full pardon from this emotional
disease and ask for total healing & deliverance
from the vicious circle & cycle of addiction to this
bondage please in the name of your Holy Son
Jesus according to John 16:23.**

Lord Jesus, son of the most high God, we ask you to
bestow your healing anointing, glory, and power
upon ___ to destroy everything that falls under the
host, characteristics, principalities, and gods of

bondage, systems of addiction, neglect, loneliness, pornography, self-pity, unemployment, laziness, procrastination, rejection, inner torment, inner hurt, the law of sin, pain, broken heart, stress, fear, & anxiety. Please conduct spiritual surgery and destroy all the signs, symptoms, and manifestations of neural brain activity within the molecular, cellular and systems-level mechanisms associated and linked to food addiction. Jesus please supply your anointing, power, and glory to deliver the signals and systems within the hippocampus organ of the brain from overeating.

We ask you Heavenly Father, for a supernatural disconnect for the Taq1A minor (A1) allele of the dopamine receptor D2 (DRD2) gene **to be unchained and unlinked** from the associations of the strongholds of alcoholism and all substance-misuse disorders, including cocaine, smoking and opioid dependence and obesity.

We also ask you Heavenly Father to hover your foot over ___ to fully terminate & remove the demonic assignments that came against ____ at the time of conception to destroy this person's life. Please shut and seal those doors forever. Everything that's leaving ___ cannot be re-assigned another demonic attack. Their banned from the planet earth and all humans, sentenced to the pit of hell until their final place in the lake of fire in the name of Jesus Christ of Nazareth.

Lord Jesus please seal ___ deliverances and this entire prayer in the power of your blood.

Heavenly Father, we ask you for total restoration of every blessing that the devil stole from ____ that ____ doesn't even know about. That this person now lives the abundant life your son Jesus Christ suffered and died for _____ to have immediately please in the name of Jesus Christ of Nazareth we pray and ask for all of these things to be done according to John 16:23 amen.

Asthma

http://www.mayoclinic.org/diseases-conditions/asthma/basics/definition/con-20026992

Asthma is a condition in which your airways narrow and swell and produce extra mucus. This can make breathing difficult and trigger coughing, wheezing and shortness of breath.

If you have asthma, *the inside walls of the airways in your lungs can become inflamed and swollen.*

In addition, *membranes in your airway linings may secrete excess mucus.*

The result is an asthma attack.

During an asthma attack, your narrowed airways make it harder to breathe and you may cough and wheeze.

http://www.mayoclinic.org/diseases-conditions/asthma-attack/multimedia/asthma-attack/img-20008649

Fight

Holy Spirit please pray with me and through me. Heavenly Father we come to you in the name of Jesus your son. I ask you to please forgive and cleanse me from all my sins. Jesus I re-dedicate my life to you and ask you to be my Savior in every area of life right now and I know, confess, and believe with all my heart that you're the Son of God.

Please equip me with the amour you know I will need to fight against the generational curse of asthma. Please enable us to operate according to the rank in your army Jesus you have called us to and grant us divine, supernatural protection for me, every one assigned, and related to me from all demonic counter-attacks.

Lord God of Heaven, we ask you for forgiveness for the persons who caused the door to the sins that caused this illness asthma, to be passed down from generation to generation.

Lord, this person was born into this curse, ____ is innocent. We ask you for a full pardon from this curse that was imputed into him/her from the time of conception and ask for total healing & deliverance please in the name of your Holy Son Jesus according to John 16:23.

Lord Jesus, son of the most high God, thou son of David, have mercy on this request, we ask you to rebuke all characteristics, effects, signs, symptoms, and manifestations of the condition in which airways narrow and swell and produce extra mucus. We also ask you to supply your anointing to destroy and annihilate all triggers (weather, allergies, & toxic environments) that make breathing difficult such as coughing, wheezing and shortness of breath.

We also ask you Heavenly Father to hover your foot over ___ to fully terminate & remove the demonic assignments that came against ____ at the time of conception to destroy this person's life. Please shut and seal those doors forever. Everything that's leaving ___ cannot be re-assigned another demonic attack. Their banned from the planet earth and all humans, sentenced to the pit of hell until their final place in the lake of fire in the name of Jesus Christ of Nazareth.

Lord Jesus please seal ___ deliverances and this entire prayer in the power of your blood.

Heavenly Father, we ask you for total restoration of every blessing that the devil stole from ____ that ____ doesn't even know about. That this person now lives the abundant life your son Jesus Christ suffered and died for ____ to have immediately please in the name of Jesus Christ of Nazareth we pray and ask for all of these things to be done according to John 16:23 amen.

Stroke

http://www.stroke.org/understand-stroke/what-stroke

A stroke is a "brain attack"

It can happen to anyone at any time.
It occurs when <u>blood flow to an area of brain is cut
off</u>. When this happens, brain cells are deprived of
oxygen and begin to die. When brain cells die during
a stroke, abilities controlled by that area of the brain
such as memory and muscle control are lost.

How a person is affected by their stroke depends on
where the stroke occurs in the brain and how much
the brain is damaged.

For example, someone who had a small stroke may
only have minor problems such as temporary
weakness of an arm or leg. People who have larger
strokes may be permanently paralyzed on one side of
their body or lose their ability to speak.

Some people recover completely from strokes, but
more than 2/3 of survivors will have some type of
disability.

Fight

Holy Spirit please pray with me and through me. Heavenly Father we come to you in the name of Jesus your son. I ask you to please forgive and cleanse me from all my sins. Jesus I re-dedicate my life to you and ask you to be my Savior in every area of life right now and I know, confess, and believe with all my heart that you're the Son of God.

Please equip me with the armor you know I will need to fight against the illness and the after effects of a stroke. Please enable us to operate according to the rank in your army Jesus you have called us to and grant us divine, supernatural protection for me, every one assigned, and related to me from all demonic counter-attacks.

Lord God of Heaven, we ask you for forgiveness for the persons who caused the door to the sins that caused the illness of stroke, to be contracted or transferred to.

We ask you for a full pardon from this infirmity and ask for total healing & deliverance please in the name of your Holy Son Jesus according to John 16:23.

Lord Jesus, son of the most high God, we ask you to bestow your healing anointing, glory, and power upon ___ to rebuke this brain attack, everything that falls under the host & god of murder, and provide a proper level of blood flow to the brain. To restore/sustain oxygen within the blood cells and to supernaturally bind back all obstructions that would attempt to cause hazardous effects of this attack.

Lord Jesus, we also pray for those who has already been victimize by this brain attack. We ask you to send an immediate response team of your angelic healing host to come and remove all the signs, symptoms, and manifestations, effects, adverse effects, stings, emotions, attacks, wrong mind sets from the stroke and also poor coordination, anxiety, memory loss, blurred vision, hearing loss, confusion, dizziness, slurred speech, unsteady walking, nausea, increased pain, loss of muscle control, loss of activity of all limbs, and all nerve & brain cell damage.

We ask you Heavenly Father, to hover your foot over ___ to fully terminate & remove the demonic distractions, hindrances, counter-attacks, and wars that would try to prevent this healing from going forth.

Everything that's leaving ___ cannot be re-assigned another specialty. Please shut and seal the door shut of the illness of stroke forever. This spirit is banned from the planet earth and all humans, sentenced to the pit of hell until their final place in the lake of fire in the name of Jesus Christ of Nazareth.

Lord Jesus please seal __ deliverances and this entire prayer in the power of your blood.

Heavenly Father, we ask you for total restoration of every blessing that the devil stole from ____ that ____ doesn't even know about. That this person now lives the abundant life your son Jesus Christ suffered and died for ____ to have immediately please in the name of Jesus Christ of Nazareth we pray and ask

for all of these things to be done according to John
16:23 amen.

Kidney Failure

- Kidneys are the organs that filter waste products from the blood. They are also involved in regulating blood pressure, electrolyte balance, and red blood cell production in the body.
- Symptoms of kidney failure are due to the build-up of waste products and excess fluid in the body that may cause weakness, shortness of breath, lethargy, swelling, and confusion. Inability to remove potassium from the bloodstream may lead to abnormal heart rhythms and sudden death. Initially kidney failure may cause no symptoms.
- There are numerous causes of kidney failure, and treatment of the underlying disease may be the first step in correcting the kidney abnormality.
- Some causes of kidney failure are treatable and the kidney function may return to normal. Unfortunately, kidney failure may be progressive in other situations and may be irreversible.
- The diagnosis of kidney failure usually is made by blood tests measuring BUN, creatinine, and glomerular filtration rate (GFR).
- Treatment of the underlying cause of kidney failure may return kidney function to normal. Lifelong efforts to control blood pressure and diabetes may be the best way to prevent

chronic <u>kidney disease</u> and its progression to kidney failure. As we age kidney function gradually decreases over time.

- If the kidneys fail completely, the only treatment options available may be <u>dialysis</u> or transplant.

Fight

Holy Spirit please pray with me and through me. Heavenly Father we come to you in the name of Jesus your son. I ask you to please forgive and cleanse me from all my sins. Jesus I re-dedicate my life to you and ask you to be my Savior in every area of life right now and I know, confess, and believe with all my heart that you're the Son of God.

Please equip me with the armor you know I will need to fight against kidney failure. Please enable us to operate according to the rank in your army Jesus you have called us to and grant us divine, supernatural protection for me, every one assigned, and related to me from all demonic counter-attacks.

Lord God of Heaven, we ask you for forgiveness for the person and people who caused the door to the sins that caused this terminal illness, kidney disease, to be transferred and contaminated with.

We ask you for a full pardon from this disease and ask for total healing & deliverance please in the name of your Holy Son Jesus according to John 16:23.

Lord Jesus, son of the most high God, we ask you to bestow your healing anointing, glory, and power upon ___ to regulate all the functions of the kidney to your optimum divine design and reverse & remove all of the effects, adverse effects, stings, wrong mind sets, emotions, and all attacks coming from kidney failure. We also ask you to supply your supernatural power to break down the build-up of waste products and excess fluid in the body that's causing weakness, shortness of breath, lethargy, swelling, confusion, and the inability to remove potassium from the bloodstream in which may cause more internal damaging effects.

We ask you Heavenly Father, to hover your foot & its power over ___ to fully terminate & remove everything that falls under the gods & hosts of infirmity and kidney abnormalities.

Please shut and seal those doors forever. Everything that's leaving ___ temple is banned from the planet earth and all humans, sentenced to the pit of hell until their final place in the lake of fire in the name of Jesus Christ of Nazareth.

Lord Jesus please seal ___ deliverances and this entire prayer in the power of your blood.

Heavenly Father, we ask you for total restoration of every blessing that the devil stole from ____ that he/she doesn't even know about. That this person now lives the abundant life your son Jesus Christ suffered and died for _____ to have immediately please in the name of Jesus Christ of Nazareth we pray and ask for all of these things to be done according to John 16:23 amen.

Liver Disease

http://www.mayoclinic.org/diseases-conditions/liver-problems/basics/definition/con-20025300

According to the Mayo Clinic, the liver is an organ about the size of a football that sits just under your rib cage on the right side of your abdomen.

The liver is essential for digesting food and ridding your body of toxic substances.

Liver disease can be <u>inherited</u> (genetic) or caused by a variety of factors that damage the liver, such as <u>viruses and alcohol use</u>.

Obesity is also associated with liver damage.

Over time, damage to the liver results in scarring (cirrhosis), which can lead to liver failure, a life-threatening condition.

Fight

Holy Spirit please pray with me and through me. Heavenly Father we come to you in the name of Jesus your son. I ask you to please forgive and cleanse me from all my sins. Jesus I re-dedicate my life to you and ask you to be my Savior in every area of life right now and I know, confess, and believe with all my heart that you're the Son of God.

Please equip me with the armor you know I will need to fight against the generational curse of liver disease. Please enable us to operate according to the rank in your army Jesus you have called us to and grant us divine, supernatural protection for me, every one assigned, and related to me from all demonic counter-attacks.

Lord God of Heaven, we ask you for forgiveness for this person and the people who caused the door to the sins of liver disease to be manifested. Lord, this person may have been born into this curse or may have come by *viruses, excessive alcohol use, and obesity*.

We ask you for a full pardon from this disease and ask for total healing & deliverance please in the name of your Holy Son Jesus according to John 16:23.

Lord Jesus, son of the most high God, we ask you to bestow your anointing, glory, and power upon ___ to correct the functions of the liver to properly rid his/her body of toxic substances & enable healthy digesting of food.

We ask you Heavenly Father, to hover your foot & its power over ___ to fully terminate & remove everything that falls under the gods & hosts of infirmity and liver disease.

Please shut and seal those doors forever. Everything that's leaving ___ temple is banned from the planet earth and all humans, sentenced to the pit of hell until their final place in the lake of fire in the name of Jesus Christ of Nazareth.

Lord Jesus please seal ___ deliverances and this entire prayer in the power of your blood.

Heavenly Father, we ask you for total restoration of every blessing that the devil stole from ____ that he/she doesn't even know about. That this person now lives the abundant life your son Jesus Christ suffered and died for _____ to have immediately please in the name of Jesus Christ of Nazareth we pray and ask for all of these things to be done according to John 16:23 amen.

Cancer

https://www.cancer.org/cancer/cancer-basics/what-is-cancer.html

According to Google, after typing a question in the search box, what is Cancer? Displayed this definition, **"the disease caused by an uncontrolled division of abnormal cells in a part of the body."** Cancer is not just one disease. There are many types of cancer. Cancer can start in the lungs, the breast, the colon, or even in the blood. Cancers are alike in some ways, but they are different in the ways they grow and spread.

http://www.cancercenter.com/what-is-cancer/

Cancer is the uncontrolled growth of abnormal cells in the body. Cancer develops when the body's normal control mechanism stops working. Old cells do not die and instead grow out of control, forming new, abnormal cells. These extra cells may form a mass of tissue, called a tumor. Some cancers, such as leukemia, do not form tumors.

There are five main categories of cancer:

- Carcinomas begin in the skin or tissues that line the internal organs.
- Sarcomas develop in the bone, cartilage, fat, muscle or other connective tissues.
- Leukemia begins in the blood and bone marrow.

- Lymphomas start in the immune system.
- Central nervous system cancers develop in the brain and spinal cord.

Fight

Holy Spirit please pray with me and through me. Heavenly Father we come to you in the name of Jesus your son. I ask you to please forgive and cleanse me from all my sins. Jesus I re-dedicate my life to you and ask you to be my Savior in every area of life right now and I know, confess, and believe with all my heart that you're the Son of God.

Please equip me with the armor you know I will need to fight against the illness & disease cancer and all its various types. Please enable us to operate according to the rank in your army Jesus you have called us to and grant us divine, supernatural protection for me, every one assigned, and related to me from all demonic counter-attacks.

Lord God of Heaven, we beg you to please forgive their sins and being unforgiving. Have mercy Lord and deliver them from everything that falls under the gods & hosts of infirmity, un-forgiveness, witchcraft, bitterness, heaviness, anger, and hatred.

IAM that IAM, we ask you for a full pardon from this disease and ask for total healing & deliverance please in the name of your Holy Son Jesus according to John 16:23.

Lord Jesus, son of the most high God, we ask you to bestow your anointing, glory, and healing power upon ___ to destroy every trace of uncontrolled growths of abnormal cells in his/her body. Restore proper functioning of the body's normal control mechanism and prevent all old cells from growing out of control, forming new, abnormal cells. Lord Jesus, son of the most high God, thou son of David, please have mercy on ___, please supply your anointing and power to destroy all old cells that need to be destroyed and never be able to return to his/her body, send your angels of healing to deliver ___ from cancer and the five main categories of it:

- Carcinomas begin in the skin or tissues that line the internal organs.
- Sarcomas develop in the bone, cartilage, fat, muscle or other connective tissues.
- Leukemia begins in the blood and bone marrow.
- Lymphomas start in the immune system.
- Central nervous system cancers develop in the brain and spinal cord.

We ask you Heavenly Father, to hover your foot & its power over ___ to fully terminate & remove everything that falls under the gods & hosts of the gods & hosts of infirmity, un-forgiveness, witchcraft, bitterness, heaviness, anger, hatred and totally disassemble, cut, sever, and destroy every cord, chains, wires, mentally unbalanced attitudes, links, roots, fruits, tentacles, spirits, and all of their signs, symptoms, manifestations, effects, adverse effects, dreams, visions, demonic imaginations, stings, wrong mind sets, emotions, and attacks that's come in him/her, coming against him/her, and in the heavens completely from all cancers and their medications.

Please shut and seal those doors forever. Everything that's leaving ___ temple is banned from the planet earth and all humans, sentenced to the pit of hell until their final place in the lake of fire in the name of Jesus Christ of Nazareth.

Lord Jesus please seal ___ deliverances and this entire prayer in the power of your blood.

Heavenly Father, we ask you for total restoration of every blessing that the devil stole from ____ that he/she doesn't even know about. That this person now lives the abundant life your son Jesus Christ suffered and died for _____ to have immediately please in the name of Jesus Christ of Nazareth we pray and ask for all of these things to be done according to John 16:23 amen.

www.ingramcontent.com/pod-product-compliance
Lightning Source LLC
Chambersburg PA
CBHW071339290326
41933CB00039B/1697